SALADIN

NOBLE PRINCE OF ISLAM

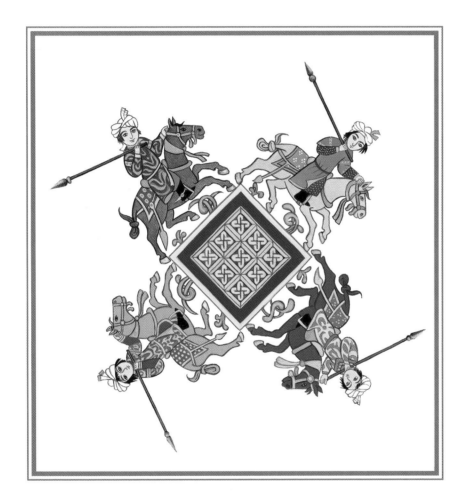

BY DIANE STANLEY

HarperCollins*Publishers*

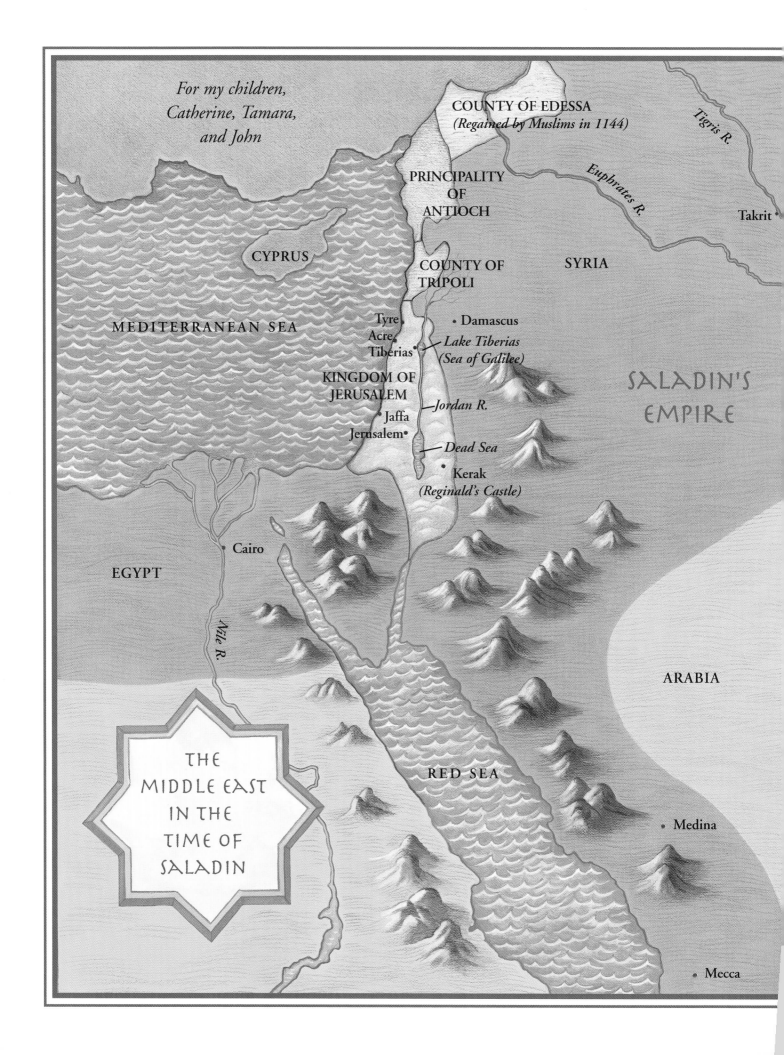

For my children,
Catherine, Tamara,
and John

COUNTY OF EDESSA
(Regained by Muslims in 1144)

Tigris R.

PRINCIPALITY
OF
ANTIOCH

Euphrates R.

Takrit •

CYPRUS

COUNTY OF
TRIPOLI

SYRIA

MEDITERRANEAN SEA

Tyre •
Acre •
Tiberias •

• Damascus

*Lake Tiberias
(Sea of Galilee)*

SALADIN'S
EMPIRE

KINGDOM OF
JERUSALEM

Jordan R.

• Jaffa

Jerusalem •

Dead Sea

• Kerak
(Reginald's Castle)

• Cairo

EGYPT

Nile R.

ARABIA

THE
MIDDLE EAST
IN THE
TIME OF
SALADIN

RED SEA

• Medina

• Mecca

People have been fighting over Jerusalem for more than three thousand years. It is called the City of David, but even King David took Jerusalem from someone else—the Jebusites—around 1000 B.C. The Jews would lose it to the Babylonians three hundred years later, and from then on the city would fall to one conqueror after another.

Over the years Jerusalem has been home to Jews, Christians, and Muslims. The followers of these three great religions, known as the People of the Book, have much in common. They worship one god and share roots in the Old Testament tradition that is central to Judaism, the most ancient of the three. They all regard Jerusalem as a holy city, and the countryside around it as the Holy Land.

By 1095 the city of Jerusalem had been in Muslim hands for more than four hundred years. The three faiths lived there together in peace, for Muhammad had taught his followers to respect Jews and Christians as "followers of an earlier revelation."

But this was soon to change. The great knights of Europe were about to embark on a holy war to drive the Muslims out of Jerusalem. Fired with religious zeal, they poured fortunes into raising armies, then transporting them—together with horses, armor, weapons, and food—two thousand miles to the Holy Land. This remarkable event came to be called the First Crusade.

By 1099 the Crusaders had conquered the coast of Syria, and on July 15 of that year they took Jerusalem. They divided the land into four Crusader States, each to be ruled by a prominent knight. Though the Muslims later reclaimed one of the states—and a Second Crusade failed to win it back—it looked like the Crusaders were in the Holy Land to stay.

In the year 1138 a boy was born in the little town of Takrit, on the Tigris River. Like every Muslim child, he was welcomed into the world of faith with these words, the first he ever heard: *"La ilaha illa Allah; Muhammad rasul Allah"*—"There is no god but Allah, and Muhammad is his Prophet."

The boy was named Yusuf ibn Ayyub, which means "Joseph, son of Job." Later he would earn a new name, Salah al-Din, "he who honors the faith."

Each morning before dawn he was awakened by the voice of the muezzin, high up in the minaret at the mosque, calling the faithful to prayer. "Prayer is better than sleep," the voice sang. The boy would wash himself as he had been taught—hands and feet, face and hair—then cover his head and turn in the direction of Mecca to pray. Four more times each day, no matter where he was—in the mosque, at the market, or at school—he would pause at the appointed times and surrender himself to God.

Religion told him what he was allowed to eat and what was forbidden, such as pork and wine. Religion decreed that for one month every year, the month of Ramadan, he was not to eat or drink anything at all from the rising of the sun until it was too dark to tell a white thread from a black one.

From the age of seven, the boy was schooled at the mosque. He memorized passages from the Koran, the holy book of Islam, and practiced writing these passages on his tablet in the beautiful Arabic script. He learned the Five Pillars of Islam—faith, prayer, the giving of alms, fasting, and pilgrimage—and knew he must follow them to be a righteous man.

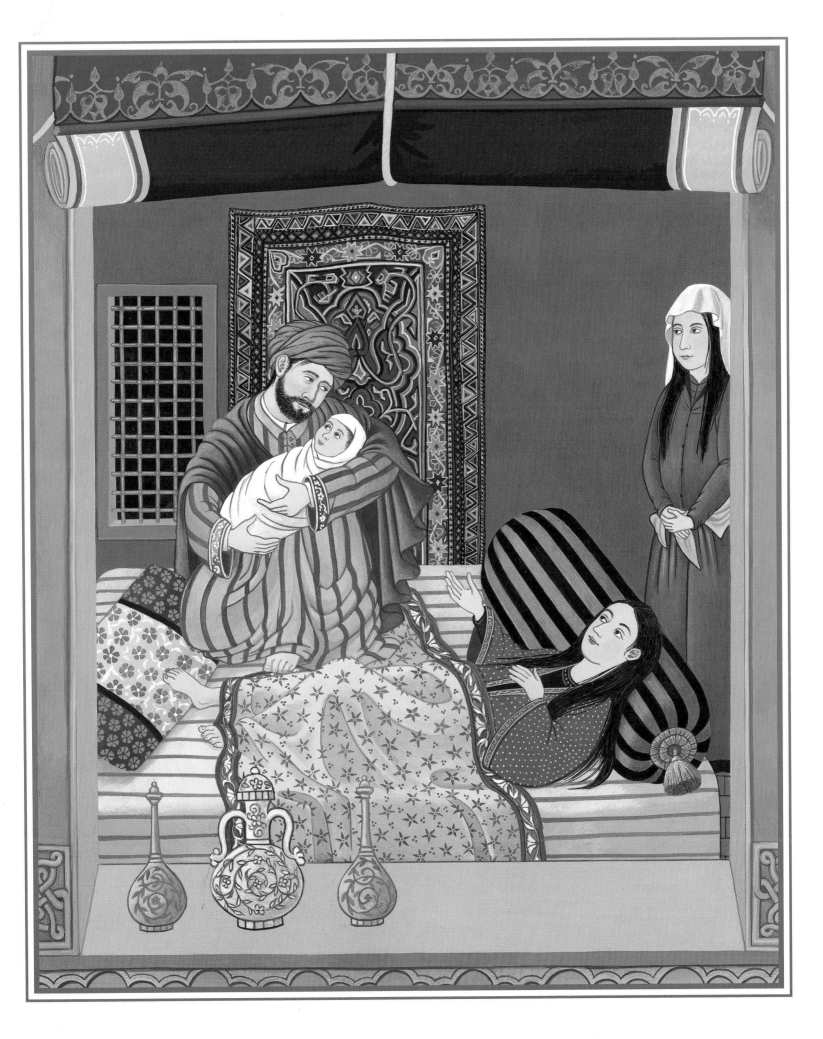

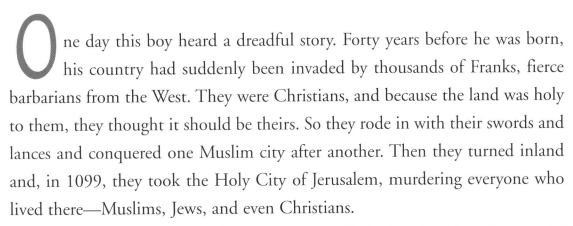

One day this boy heard a dreadful story. Forty years before he was born, his country had suddenly been invaded by thousands of Franks, fierce barbarians from the West. They were Christians, and because the land was holy to them, they thought it should be theirs. So they rode in with their swords and lances and conquered one Muslim city after another. Then they turned inland and, in 1099, they took the Holy City of Jerusalem, murdering everyone who lived there—Muslims, Jews, and even Christians.

The boy could scarcely believe it. How could the Franks think God would send anyone on such a terrible mission? Didn't they know that Muslims and Jews also worshipped the God of Abraham and called Jerusalem holy? It was the city where David had built the Hebrew Temple. It was the place where Jesus spent his final days. The beautiful Dome of the Rock marked the sacred spot where the prophet Muhammad was carried up into heaven and beheld the face of God. And Jerusalem was where the Muslim faithful would gather on the Last Day. Couldn't everyone just share it?

Yet the story was true. That beautiful city, holy to three faiths, was now the capital of the Kingdom of Jerusalem, ruled by coarse men who could scarcely read or write and who thought it unhealthy to take a bath. They were valiant fighters, though. It would not be easy to drive them out.

What the boy felt as he pondered all this, we can only imagine. Like other boys of his time, he must have dreamed of riding off to war and sending those horrible men scurrying back to France or England—or wherever it was they had come from. But unlike those other boys, he would actually do it. One day he would become famous as Saladin, the Muslim saint-king, praised even by his enemies as "the marvel of his time."

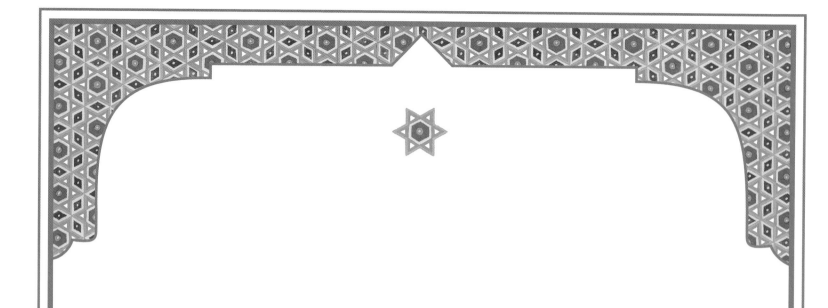

Saladin and his family had left Takrit when he was just a baby. They traveled west and settled in the territory of the great Turkish sultan Nur al-Din, who ruled his growing empire from the capital at Damascus. Though Saladin's family were Kurds and spoke the Kurdish language, they quickly learned Arabic and rose to high positions in the sultan's service—his father as governor of Damascus and his uncle as a powerful general. They used their connections to help Saladin get a good start in life.

When Saladin was fourteen, he joined Nur al-Din's army, and a few years later he became the sultan's chief aide. Being constantly at the side of this extraordinary man was more than just a privilege—it was an education in how to be a righteous man. Though Nur al-Din was wealthy and powerful, he chose to live a simple life and devote his riches to the welfare of his people. He was devout, generous, and fair, believing that every man was equal before God and before the law. Saladin saw his master as an ideal prince and made Nur al-Din his model. He took on the sultan's dream as well as his ways, for Nur al-Din imagined a day when the Muslims would stop fighting one another and unite against the Christian invaders.

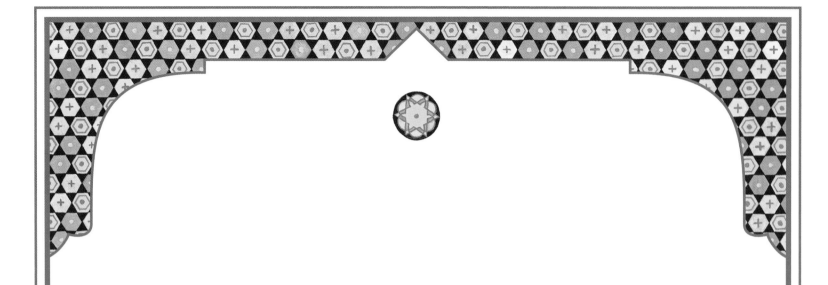

When he was in his late twenties, Saladin traveled three times to Egypt with Nur al-Din's army, under the command of his uncle Shirkuh. The third visit proved to be a turning point in his life.

Egypt was in political chaos at the time. Because of its weakness and great wealth, Egypt was seen by the Franks as a juicy plum, ripe for the picking. Nur al-Din took the same view. The vizier—or ruler—of Egypt began playing the Franks against the Turks, alternately asking one to protect him from the other. This strategy worked admirably until the day when Shirkuh, having repeatedly driven the Franks out of Egypt, simply refused to go home. The vizier decided to rid himself of his unwanted guest by having Shirkuh assassinated.

Instead it was the vizier who lost his life. The caliph, the religious leader of Egypt, had him executed and put Shirkuh in his place. This stunning turn of affairs was soon followed by another: nine weeks after his appointment Shirkuh died, and Saladin became vizier of Egypt.

It was an astonishing and unexpected rise to power—but it put Saladin in an awkward position. He was ruling territory that had been captured by Nur al-Din's army and that was now part of his empire. Saladin insisted that he was not making a grab for power and that he still served Nur al-Din; but back in Damascus they called him a "dog that barks at its master."

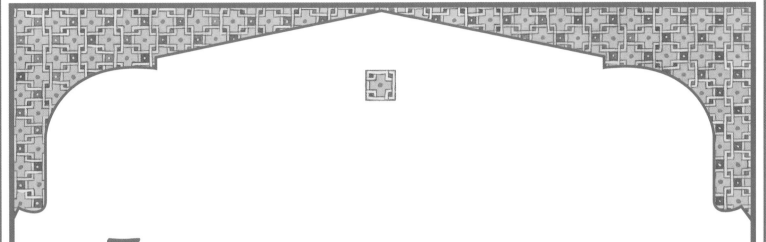

Three years later Nur al-Din died. His heir was a boy of eleven, clearly too young to rule an empire. None of Nur al-Din's quarrelsome brothers had any gift for leadership. Saladin believed he was the only one who could keep the empire together and use it for the great purpose Nur al-Din had intended, so he marched an army into Syria and staked his claim to the empire.

Nur al-Din's brothers were not about to give in to Saladin, and for the next nine years they were almost constantly at war with one another. But Saladin never forgot that the men he was fighting were his fellow Muslims and that someday they would be fighting side by side against the Christians. So he ordered his soldiers to treat the enemy as brothers: there was to be no looting or burning. They were never to pursue an army that was retreating. And captives were to be treated generously.

By 1185 Saladin had finally made peace with the last of Nur al-Din's brothers. It was the perfect time to launch his holy war against the Franks, for the Crusader States were in chaos, divided into two warring factions over who should be king of Jerusalem.

On one side were men whose families had lived in the East for many generations and had learned to respect Muslim ways. Their leader was the wise and capable Raymond of Tripoli. The other party, mostly warlike newcomers, was led by Reginald of Châtillon, perhaps the greatest villain in the history of the Crusades. Unfortunately for the Christians, Reginald's faction won out and his candidate, the haughty, incompetent Guy of Lusignan, was crowned king.

Saladin didn't take advantage of this golden opportunity for reasons of honor. Back in 1184 when he had been fighting his fellow Muslims, Saladin had signed a four-year truce with the Franks. Though it would have been convenient to ignore that truce now, Saladin never went back on his word. But Reginald of Châtillon had no such qualms. Just when the Franks could least afford to go to war, he broke the truce himself.

Reginald had come to Syria as a young man. Having no money or estates in Europe, he had managed to acquire them in the East through marriage to not one but two wealthy widows. By the time Saladin was conquering Muslim Syria, Reginald had become master of Kerak, one of the strongest castles in the kingdom, overlooking the caravan routes from Cairo and Mecca to Damascus.

In those days Arab caravans passed freely through Frankish lands, just as Frankish merchants did through Syria. It was a good arrangement that made trade and travel safe for everyone. But Reginald made his own rules. He liked to pounce on peaceful caravans passing near his castle. On one notorious occasion he launched a fleet of pirate ships that raided coastal towns along the Red Sea, attacking pilgrims on their way to Mecca. Reginald even tried to kidnap the body of the Prophet Muhammad from his tomb in Medina and hold it in his castle for ransom. The venture failed, but the attempt was enough to make him the most hated man in Syria.

Now Reginald spotted a rich caravan on its way back from Mecca. With no apparent concern for the consequences, he attacked it, killing the escorts, robbing the merchants of their goods, and taking the pilgrims captive. The Franks would soon pay a heavy price for that brutal and reckless act.

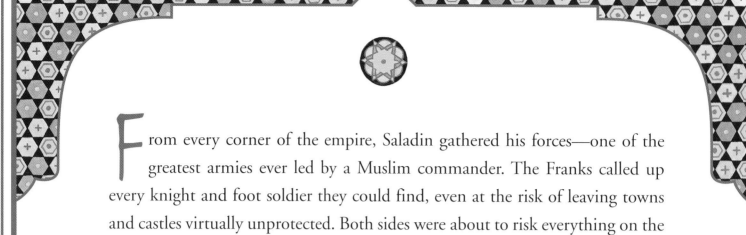

From every corner of the empire, Saladin gathered his forces—one of the greatest armies ever led by a Muslim commander. The Franks called up every knight and foot soldier they could find, even at the risk of leaving towns and castles virtually unprotected. Both sides were about to risk everything on the outcome of a single battle.

Saladin believed that the Franks' greatest weakness was their leader, King Guy of Jerusalem. He was said to be a bit of a fool, easily led by hotheaded knights like Reginald. Such a man could be counted on to make a reckless move if he thought his honor was at stake. And this is exactly what Saladin was counting on.

In July of 1187 Saladin attacked Tiberias, the castle of Raymond of Tripoli. Raymond was away with the army, but his wife was there with a small garrison of soldiers. As the Turks broke through the outer walls, she took refuge in the citadel and sent a messenger to the Christian camp with a plea for help.

That night a council was held in King Guy's tent to decide what to do. Guy was eager to rush to the countess's aid, but Raymond argued against it. If there was one thing he had learned from years of fighting in the Holy Land, it was never to get too far from walls or water. To reach Tiberias, the army would have to cross a waterless desert plateau in the heat of summer, and they might not make it. It was, he reminded them, *his* castle and *his* wife that were threatened. But he would rather see his castle destroyed and his wife enslaved than lose the entire army—and with it, the kingdom.

By the time the council broke up for the night, Guy had accepted the wisdom of giving up Tiberias. But several knights remained behind in the tent after the others left. Without Raymond there to talk sense to the king, he was easily convinced to change his mind. They had fallen into Saladin's trap.

They were in Raymond's territory, so by custom it was he who rode—with a heavy heart—at the head of the greatest army the Crusaders had ever mobilized. Behind him came more than 1,200 mounted knights and another 10,000 foot soldiers. In the center, with King Guy, rode two bishops carrying the Sacred Relic of the True Cross—said to be a fragment of the actual cross on which Jesus was crucified. People in the Middle Ages were very fond of such relics, and many had been discovered in the Holy Land—from the original Crown of Thorns to the bottled tears of Jesus. But the True Cross was the Christians' most prized and holy object and was believed to have powers to protect them in battle. Sadly, they were about to lose it.

Guy had made the unfortunate decision not to bring along an extra supply of water. Each soldier was responsible for carrying his own. For hours the army marched under the blistering sun, haunted by the beating of Muslim drums and harassed by a steady stream of mounted archers who showered them with arrows. The Turks were like "an irritating fly," one Christian chronicler wrote. "If you drive it off, it will leave you. But when you desist, it returns." The men grew exhausted from the strain. They were baking inside their heavy armor, and many had no water left. With the rear guard falling behind in their effort to fight off the pursuing Turks (while marching backward), Guy called a halt.

When Raymond heard the order, he was horrified. Their only chance was to keep going in hopes of reaching Lake Tiberias. "Alas!" he is said to have cried. "The war is over! We are betrayed to death and the land is lost."

There was little rest in the Christian camp that night. Saladin's troops surrounded it so tightly that, as one witness later wrote, not even a cat could have escaped. All night the sky rained arrows on the Franks' heads. Scorpions and tarantulas crawled into their clothes. And by the light of the campfires, the thirsty Franks had to watch as the Turks gaily poured gallons of precious water into the sand.

The next morning the Franks resumed their formation and continued marching east, toward Tiberias. Saladin set grass fires at strategic spots along the way where the wind would blow the smoke in their direction. The Franks, already weak and suffering from thirst, plodded forward with the rising sun in their faces and smoke stinging their eyes.

Finally, on a rocky plateau between two mountains known as the Horns of Hattin, Guy called a halt and ordered his men to prepare for battle. With the king's red tent as a rallying point, the Franks threw themselves into the fray with astonishing courage. But "no matter how hard they fought, they were repulsed," one Muslim witness wrote. "No matter how often they rallied, each time they were encircled. . . . Fate tore at them; calamity chewed them up." When the king's tent fell, so did the last hopes of the Christian army. King Guy and the greatest knights of the land were taken captive. So many soldiers were sold into slavery after the Battle of Hattin that prices on the slave market plummeted. And the Relic of the True Cross fell into Muslim hands and was lost forever.

Raymond was one of the few knights to escape the disaster he had tried so hard to prevent. But it gave him no joy. Only a few weeks later, as the Kingdom of Jerusalem was falling bit by bit to Saladin's army, this most noble Frankish knight died at Tripoli. Some said he died of shame.

After the battle Saladin summoned the most prominent captives to his tent. With the politeness of a gracious host, he offered King Guy a goblet of water, cooled by snow. This gesture of hospitality meant that Saladin had decided to spare Guy's life, for by Eastern custom no captive who shared food or drink with his captor could then be killed. Guy innocently passed the cup on to Reginald. At this, Saladin grew angry. "It was not *I* who gave you that drink," he said—for though he took no pleasure in bloodshed, Saladin had no intention of sparing Reginald.

With no army left to oppose him, Saladin now moved to reclaim his land. He began with Tiberias, where he released Raymond's wife and had her politely escorted to safety. Then, one by one, the Frankish cities surrendered. There were no bloodbaths; there was no looting. The defeated soldiers were allowed to buy their freedom and take their treasure with them.

Soon a steady stream of refugees was pouring into the fortress at Tyre, where the few survivors of Hattin had fled. The city now became the center of Christian resistance (such as it was), and Saladin should have taken it right away. But he went after easier targets first, a grave mistake. In that crucial window of time, Conrad of Montferrat sailed into the harbor at Tyre with a small band of soldiers. He was just the leader the Franks needed. They greeted him with almost hysterical joy and immediately put him in charge of the defense. From that moment all talk of surrender ceased.

Tyre should have been an easy conquest for Saladin. But now it would mean a long, hard siege. So Saladin turned away from Tyre, planning to deal with it later. With most of Syria back in Muslim hands, he felt the time had come to put the jewel in the crown—he would take back Jerusalem.

While Saladin was getting ready for his assault on the Holy City, he received a message from an important knight named Balian, one of the survivors of Hattin. Counting on Saladin's famous generosity, Balian asked permission to travel through enemy lines to bring his wife and children out of Jerusalem before the siege started. Saladin agreed to this request—if Balian promised to stay only one night and not take part in the fighting. Balian gave his oath.

But when he arrived and saw how desperate the situation was, he was torn. The fighting forces of the city consisted of two knights and a population of merchants, women, children, priests, nuns, and peasants. It was clearly his Christian duty to stay and take command. So Balian wrote again to Saladin, explaining his dilemma. The reply amazed the Christians: not only did Saladin release the knight from his sworn oath—he even arranged for the man's wife and children to be escorted to safety. And so Balian stayed to prepare a heroic—though hopeless—defense.

Saladin had hoped for a peaceful surrender. "I believe that Jerusalem is the House of God," he wrote to Balian, "as you also believe. And I will not willingly lay siege to the House of God or put it to the assault." He offered extraordinarily generous terms of surrender, but they were rejected. Saladin would have to take the city by force.

He had with him forty mangonels, giant siege engines that relentlessly hurled stones against the city walls and onto the battlements. At the same time a tunnel was dug under the walls, supported by wooden beams. When it was complete, the tunnel was filled with brush and set on fire. As the supports burned, the tunnel collapsed, and with it came the wall. On October 2, 1187, two weeks after Saladin first laid siege to Jerusalem, the city surrendered.

The Muslims had never forgotten the shocking massacre that marked the Christian takeover of Jerusalem back in 1099. Yet Saladin did not seek revenge. He posted guards around the city to make sure his soldiers behaved in an orderly and respectful manner. Even the Christian chroniclers admit that none of their people was mistreated.

As was customary in those days, Saladin allowed the people of Jerusalem to buy their freedom. They were given forty days to raise their ransom. Each man had to pay ten dinars, almost a year's wages for a laborer. Women had to pay five dinars, and children only one. But there were thousands of people in the city who were simply too poor to pay. It would be nice to write here that the head of the church in Jerusalem, the patriarch Eraclius, did all he could to raise money to help these unfortunate Christians. But sadly the patriarch paid only his own ransom, then carried off cartloads of treasure from the church—gold and silver candlesticks, chalices, icons, tapestries, and carpets—which, if sold, could have ransomed thousands. The Muslims were appalled by "this unholy man."

Saladin's brother asked for a thousand poor captives as a gift, then gave them their freedom. Saladin responded to this chivalrous gesture by freeing all of the elderly poor. There were so many of these that one witness said it took an entire day for them to leave the city. The captives who remained were sent to the slave market in Damascus.

As the last of the Franks left Jerusalem and the Muslims set about purifying their holy places, Saladin must have felt enormous joy. His great dream had been accomplished. Now the only "arrow left in the quiver of the infidels" was Tyre, and once it surrendered, Saladin would rule over a Muslim empire, united and at peace.

The news that Jerusalem was lost arrived in Rome on a ship with black sails—the ancient symbol of bad tidings. It caused a wave of hysteria throughout Europe. Pope Urban III was said to have died from the shock. The new pope, Gregory VIII, called for a Third Crusade.

Immediately the kings of Germany and France took the cross. So did King Richard I of England—the most fearsome opponent Saladin would ever face. To finance this mighty effort, Richard levied a 10 percent tax on the possessions of all persons, called the "Saladin tithe." Elevating his fund-raising to a new level, Richard fired his public officers, then made them buy their jobs back. "I would sell London," he said, "if I could find a buyer for it."

Conrad just needed to hold on to Tyre—the remaining Christian foothold in the Holy Land—until the Crusaders could get there. For two months Saladin tried valiantly to take the city, but it was the strongest fortress in the kingdom and he was having no success. By December the rain and cold had set in. Muslim armies rarely fought in the winter, and Saladin's men were near rebellion. Unaware that the armed might of Europe was about to descend upon him, Saladin disbanded his army for the winter.

At about that time, Saladin gave King Guy his freedom. The king hurried to Tyre, where he discovered to his astonishment that Conrad had barred the gates against him. It seemed that Conrad wanted the crown for himself.

Since Guy couldn't use Tyre as his base, he headed south with his small band of supporters and laid siege to Acre. It was laughable. The Muslims outnumbered the Franks two to one, and they had strong walls to protect them. And Guy had already proved what kind of leader he was. Saladin found it hard to take the whole thing seriously.

By the time Saladin finally got to Acre, reinforcements had started arriving from Europe. The Christian camp was so well dug in and its defenses so strong that Saladin could not budge them. The result was one of the most bizarre sieges in history. The Muslims were inside, defending the city; Guy's army was outside, besieging it; and beyond that—spread out across the hills and plains—was Saladin's army, besieging the besiegers. And that's how they would remain, fighting ferociously, for 638 days.

As the months passed, food grew scarce in the Christian camp. Typhus was rampant, and more soldiers died of disease than in battle. Then in the spring of 1191, the armies of the Third Crusade reached Acre. First came Philip Augustus of France, followed a few weeks later by the dashing king of England, Richard the Lion-Hearted. These two warlike rulers had taken a break from fighting each other to go on Crusade together and fight the infidel.

Richard grew up in one of the most dysfunctional families in history—historians call them "the devil's brood." His father, Henry II, fought with his sons (literally, with armies), and the sons fought one another. Henry threw his wife, Eleanor of Acquitaine, into prison and only named Richard heir to the throne because he was forced to do so on the battlefield. At the ceremony, instead of giving the customary kiss, Henry whispered into his son's ear, "God grant that I may not die until I have had my revenge on you." It's no wonder Richard turned out to be an obnoxious bully with a genius for making enemies.

But for all that, Richard was a brilliant commander who justly deserved the name Lion-Hearted for his enormous courage. No one questioned that he should be given the supreme command. And indeed, he had been at Acre scarcely a month when the city surrendered.

The commanders at Acre had not consulted Saladin on the terms of their surrender. Yet he was the one who would have to raise the 200,000 gold pieces and locate the 1,500 Christian prisoners to be released. Until he had met these terms, the garrison at Acre would be held prisoner.

Saladin was not able to raise that much money in the time allowed, and some of the specifically named prisoners couldn't be located. So when the appointed day arrived, not all the terms had been met. Richard was furious—his campaign was at a standstill while he was stuck at Acre, minding his hostages. So, with a cold-bloodedness that stunned the Muslim world, he had the prisoners roped together and led out of the city, then ordered the systematic slaughter of all three thousand men.

This shocking display of cruelty made a big impression on the Muslims. From that time on, soldiers defending cities against Richard were inclined to surrender—for the rules of war dictated that a surrendering army should be spared. But if they put up a fight and lost, Richard could not be counted on to be generous, as Saladin had been at Jerusalem.

Even after Richard left the Holy Land, his image lingered in the people's imagination as a sort of bogeyman. Muslim parents would scold their naughty children by saying, "You behave, or I'll set the king of England on you!"

Richard soon had the whole Crusade to himself. The king of Germany had never reached Acre, having died on the way. Now the king of France decided to leave after only two months. Apparently that was all the time in Richard's company that Philip could stand. Pleading illness, he sailed for France, leaving most of his troops behind.

At the end of August 1191 Richard marched his army south toward Jaffa. It was a trek of some eighty miles with eight rivers to cross, and the men were under constant attack by Saladin's archers. Richard had to keep his troops together and restrain their natural desire to break out of formation and chase the Turks. It was a true test of Richard's leadership.

In the Middle Ages the greatest strength of a western army was a mass charge of armored knights. But a knight was useless without his horse, and the Turkish archers had quickly discovered this weakness. So knights always rode between columns of foot soldiers, who acted as human shields for the horses while at the same time keeping the Turks at bay with their crossbows. With chain mail under their surcoats, the infantrymen were well protected from Muslim fire. They were sometimes seen marching along with dozens of arrows sticking out of their backs, like an army of oversized hedgehogs.

Saladin had hoped that heat and exhaustion would weaken the Christian troops and make his job easier, as it had at Hattin. But Richard was a far better commander than Guy. He divided his infantry into two groups, alternating their days in the line of fire with days of marching along the beach, safe from the attacking Turks. They traveled only in the mornings and rested every other day.

In fact it was Saladin's army that was weakening. Exhausted from years of constant fighting, they faced troops fresh from Europe, led by a brilliant commander. So when Saladin finally attacked the Franks, it was a disaster. Disheartened Muslim soldiers galloped away from the charging knights in utter confusion. "All our men were wounded," one witness wrote, "if not in their bodies, then in their hearts."

Saladin could not keep Richard from taking the rest of the coastal cities, so he hurried to Jerusalem and began to strengthen its defenses. Then he waited for the terrifying Richard to fall upon them. It was January, and the weather turned stormy and cold. The Frankish soldiers began dying of exposure and disease. "So great was the tempest and such the downpour of rain and showers," one chronicler wrote, "that the stakes of [our] tents were torn up and whirled away, whilst our horses perished of cold and wet." It must have been clear to Richard that his army was not up to a prolonged siege under those conditions.

Saladin had already manned the battlements for the expected attack when a messenger came galloping up with amazing news: the Franks had halted—almost within sight of Jerusalem—and held a big meeting. Then they had turned back!

Richard spent the rest of that terrible winter trying to keep the Crusade from turning into a civil war between the forces of Conrad and Guy. Then, as if things weren't bad enough, Richard received shocking news from England: his brother John, whom he had left in charge while he was gone, had been conspiring with his old enemy, King Philip of France, to seize his lands. Richard had no choice but to go home.

But before he left, Richard marched once more on Jerusalem. There is a legend that as the army neared the city, Richard climbed the hill where, a hundred years before, the Crusaders had first spied Jerusalem. But Richard held up his shield to block the precious sight. "God, I pray thee not to let me see thy Holy City," Richard said, "[if I cannot] deliver it out of the hands of thy enemies." And indeed, aware that he lacked the manpower to hold Jerusalem, even should he be able to take it, Richard once again turned away from the Holy City he had come so far to recapture—and now would never see.

The Third Crusade had run its course. Negotiations for a truce, which had been proceeding halfheartedly for some time, now grew serious, with Saladin's brother acting as intermediary. Richard and Saladin, the towering figures of their age, never actually met face-to-face.

Though Richard had shown he was the superior commander, Saladin had some advantages that strengthened his position. He was in the heart of his own country, surrounded by family and friends. And while Richard had other concerns back in England, this war was Saladin's whole life. "The land was ours to begin with," Saladin wrote, "and ye invaded it. . . . I will not give up until God grants the victory to whosoever he willeth."

On September 2, 1192, a truce was signed that was to last for three years. The Franks would keep the strip of coastline from Tyre to Jaffa. The rest, including Jerusalem, would belong to the Muslims. Before the Crusaders left, Saladin allowed them to travel safely to Jerusalem and make their pilgrimages to the holy places. But Richard refused to go. God had not granted him victory over the city in the Christian cause; he would not go there as the guest of a Muslim king.

Richard made it clear that he was only leaving for a while. He needed time to set his kingdom to rights and raise a new army. Then he would return and take back the whole kingdom. Saladin replied to this boast with a gracious message: he said if he had to lose his land, he would rather lose it to Richard than to anybody else.

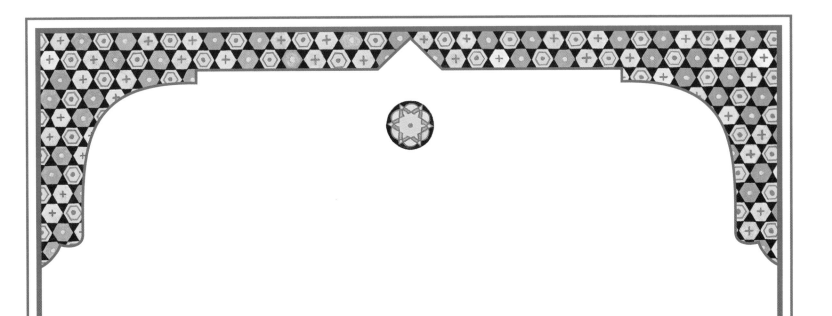

Saladin returned home to Damascus for the first time in four years, grateful to be with his family again. Sadly, we know almost nothing about his married life. Women and girls are almost totally absent from the history of that time and place.

We do know that when Saladin was first making his claim to be Nur al-Din's successor, he married the great man's widow, Ismat. It was a political marriage, of course, yet Saladin came to care deeply for Ismat. He was not able to see her often, for he was usually away with the army, yet he took the time to write her long letters every day. When she died, Saladin was lying in his tent, seriously ill. His advisors kept the news from him for three months, until he was fully recovered, for fear the shock might kill him.

After years of rough living in the company of soldiers, Saladin settled into a gentler life in Damascus. Though Ismat was gone, we assume he had other wives—for Muslim men are allowed to have four. It is said he spent much of his time with his children, going hunting with his older boys and playing happily with the little ones.

He considered making his pilgrimage to Mecca, the birthplace of Muhammad, but put it off. He could not have known that the thread of his life would soon be cut.

Saladin was not feeling well, but he rode out in bad weather to join the festivities that traditionally welcomed a caravan of pilgrims back from Mecca. The next morning he awoke with a fever. As the days passed and he grew steadily weaker, it was clear that he was dying.

On March 4, 1193, Saladin lay unconscious with a holy man beside him, reading from the Koran. "He is God, besides whom there is no other God," the man read, "who knoweth the unseen and the seen, the Compassionate, the Merciful." Saladin awoke and said softly, "True." They were his last words. The reader continued: "In Him do I trust." At that, Saladin is said to have smiled and passed peacefully into death.

Before he died, Saladin had called his oldest son to his bedside and given him this advice on how to be a king: "Win the hearts of your people and watch over their prosperity; for it is to secure their happiness that you are appointed by God and by me. . . . I have become as great as I am because I have won men's hearts by gentleness and kindness."

Saladin had never cared for money or luxury. Whatever riches had come to him he had given away, so that there was not even enough money left to pay for his simple burial.

The people of Damascus were overcome with grief. A physician in Damascus observed that it was the only case he knew of where a king's death was truly mourned. Saladin, he wrote, had been "a great prince, whose appearance inspired both respect and love, who was approachable, deeply intellectual, gracious, and noble in his thoughts. All who came near him took him as their model." He would be a model for any age.

Without Saladin's leadership, his empire soon broke up into a patchwork of semi-independent states, ruled by his descendants. For the next fifty-six years they would sometimes pull together for the common cause and at other times make war on one another. Though the empire never again reached the heights it had in Saladin's time, the region remained in Muslim hands and achieved a measure of stability in troubled times.

Richard never returned to the Holy Land—nor did he get back to England any time soon. Disliking long sea voyages, he chose the overland route, which took him through the territory of several bitter enemies. Traveling in disguise as a merchant named Hugh, Richard had reached Austria when his identity was discovered. Unfortunately for Richard, the land belonged to a certain Duke Leopold whom Richard had boorishly insulted at Acre by having the duke's banner taken down and trampled in the dust. Now Leopold got his revenge.

Richard was sitting in a dungeon when he learned of Saladin's death. And there Richard would remain for two years, held for a "king's ransom" of 100,000 gold marks. Richard's old enemy, King Philip of France, actually offered a greater sum to *keep* him in prison, but the offer was refused.

To raise Richard's ransom, a heavy tax was laid on the English people. It had been only four years since they had paid the "Saladin tithe" to fund the Crusade. Now the kingdom was practically bankrupt. Burdened by poverty and corruption, the people dreamed of a champion who would take their side against the rich and powerful—and the legend of Robin Hood was born.

Richard was finally freed and spent the rest of his life at war with France, managing to regain most of the land Philip had stolen. In 1199 he was killed while besieging a castle and was succeeded by his unfaithful brother John.

The dispute between Conrad and Guy ended with neither man winning the throne. Guy was still technically king, but the army no longer trusted him after the disaster at Hattin. So Richard reluctantly gave Conrad his support, compensating Guy by making him king of Cyprus. It is said that Conrad piously prayed to God that he might not become king of Jerusalem unless he was truly worthy of the honor. Evidently he wasn't, for before he could be crowned, Conrad was murdered. With both candidates now out of the running, the throne went instead to Richard's nephew, Henry of Champagne.

The Franks managed to hold on to their small strip of coastline for another hundred years, during which time there were five more Crusades. Though all of them failed, the Fourth Crusade was undoubtedly the low point. Having set out to regain Jerusalem, the Crusaders got sidetracked and ended up sacking and burning Constantinople, the great capital of Orthodox Christianity. In 1291 the Franks were driven out of the Holy Land altogether.

For the Christians, the Crusades had been a complete disaster. Thousands of lives had been lost and fortunes squandered—yet the Muslims still held the Holy Land. Not only had the Crusaders failed to accomplish their goal, they had done immeasurable harm. Two hundred years of Frankish invasion, senseless slaughter, and religious fanaticism left a tragic legacy. A shadow of hatred and mistrust had fallen over this great land, holy to three faiths. A thousand years later, it is still there.

Arabs—The original inhabitants of the Arabian Peninsula. After converting to Islam, the Arabs spread widely throughout the Middle East, North Africa, southern Europe, and beyond. Though by Saladin's time the Holy Land had been conquered by Turks, the majority of the people living there were Arabs. Most were Muslims, but there were also Arab Christians. All were united by a common language, Arabic.

caliph—A Muslim religious leader and supreme ruler, regarded as a successor to Muhammad.

chroniclers—The people who wrote down the details of historical events of their time. Firsthand accounts survive from both the Muslim and Christian sides during the Crusades and are the source for much of the information and all of the direct quotes in this book.

Franks—A Germanic tribe that once ruled much of Europe. By Saladin's time, they had lost large portions of their empire and had settled in the general region known today as France. Though the Crusaders came from many countries and spoke various languages, to the Muslims they were all "Franks." Similarly, the Crusaders referred to all Muslims—whether Turks or Arabs—as "Saracen."

infidel—Derived from a Latin word meaning "disloyal." An infidel is someone who does not follow a certain religion or has no religion at all. Both Muslims and Christians used the word to describe the other.

Islam—A religion founded by the prophet Muhammad. The Muslim era officially dates from A.D. 622, when Muhammad and his followers fled from Mecca to Medina, an event known as the *Hijra*. Muslims worship one god, revere the Hebrew prophets and Jesus, and consider Muhammad to be the last and greatest prophet.

Koran (alternately, *Quran*)—The sacred text of Islam, containing the word of God as revealed to the prophet Muhammad.

Kurds—A seminomadic people from the mountains of southwestern Asia. They converted to Islam when their lands were conquered by the Arabs in the seventh century. By Saladin's time, Kurdish lands were under the control of the Turks.

mangonel—A large apparatus for flinging stones and other large missiles at the defensive walls of castles and fortresses during sieges.

Mecca—The holiest city in Islam, birthplace of Muhammad. It is the duty of every Muslim to make a pilgrimage, or *hajj*, to Mecca, if at all possible.

Medina—The second-holiest city in Islam, the place where Muhammad and his followers settled after they fled from Mecca in 622. The tomb of Muhammad is in Medina.

mosque—A Muslim house of worship.

muezzin—The person who calls Muslims to prayer five times a day, usually from a high tower, called a *minaret*, at a mosque.

Muslim (alternately, *Moslem*)—One who follows the faith of Islam. From the Arabic word meaning "one who surrenders" to God.

siege—The surrounding of a city or fortress by an army in an effort to subdue it. The siege was the most common method of fighting in the Middle Ages, pitched battles being very rare.

Turks—A nomadic people from central Asia who conquered large parts of the Middle East and the northern coast of Africa, adopting the Muslim religion from the Arabs they displaced. The modern country of Turkey, part of the territory the Turks once ruled, was named after them.

vizier—The chief minister or other high officer in a Muslim government. In Saladin's time, the vizier of Egypt had unusual powers. Though he was appointed by the true ruler, the caliph, the vizier actually ran the government.

BIBLIOGRAPHY

Armstrong, Karen. *Islam: A Short History.* New York: Modern Library, 2000.

———. *Jerusalem: One City, Three Faiths.* New York: Ballantine Books, 1997.

Ehrenkreutz, Andrew S. *Saladin.* Albany: State University of New York Press, 1972.

Gibb, Sir Hamilton. *Saladin: Studies in Islamic History.* Ed. Yusuf Ibish. Beirut: Arab Institute for Research and Publishing, 1974.

Hallam, Elizabeth, ed. *Chronicles of the Crusades.* New York: Weidenfeld and Nicolson, 1989.

Hillenbrand, Carole. *The Crusades: Islamic Perspectives.* Chicago: Fitzroy Dearborn Publishers, 1999.

Kedar, B. Z., ed. *The Horns of Hattin.* Jerusalem: Yad Izhak Ben-Zvi, 1992.

Lane-Poole, Stanley. *Saladin and the Fall of the Kingdom of Jerusalem.* Beirut: Khayats, 1964.

Maalouf, Amin. *The Crusades Through Arab Eyes.* Trans. Jon Rothschild. New York: Schocken Books, 1984.

Newby, P. H. *Saladin in His Time.* Boston and London: Faber and Faber, 1983.

Regan, Geoffrey. *Lionhearts: Richard I, Saladin, and the Era of the Third Crusade.* New York: Walker and Company, 1998.

Reston, Jr., James. *Warrior of God: Richard the Lionheart and Saladin in the Third Crusade.* New York: Doubleday, 2001.

Riley-Smith, Jonathan, ed. *The Oxford Illustrated History of the Crusades.* Oxford and New York: Oxford University Press, 1995.

Stewart, Desmond. *Early Islam.* New York: Time, 1967.

Tate, Georges. *The Crusaders: Warriors of God.* New York: Harry N. Abrams, 1996.

Usamah ibn Munqidh. *An Arab-Syrian Gentleman and Warrior in the Period of the Crusades; Memoirs of Usamah ibn Munqidh (Kitab al-i'tibar).* Translated from the original manuscript by Philip K. Hitti. New York: Columbia University Press, 1929.

The author wishes to thank Richard W. Bulliet, Professor of History, Middle East Institute, Columbia University, for his helpful review of the text and illustrations.

Saladin • Copyright © 2002 by Diane Stanley • Printed in the U.S.A. All rights reserved.
www.harperchildrens.com • Library of Congress Cataloging-in-Publication Data • Stanley, Diane.
Saladin : Noble Prince of Islam / by Diane Stanley. • p.   cm. • Includes bibliographical references.
ISBN 0-688-17135-4—ISBN 0-688-17136-2 (lib. bdg.) • 1. Saladin, Sultan of Egypt and Syria,
1137–1193—Juvenile literature. 2. Egypt—Kings and rulers—Biography—Juvenile literature.
3. Syria—Kings and rulers—Biography—Juvenile literature. 4. Crusades—Juvenile literature.
[1. Saladin, Sultan of Egypt and Syria, 1137–1193. 2. Kings, queens, rulers, etc. 3. Crusades.]
I. Title. DS38.4.S2 S83 2002 956'.014'092—dc21   2001024636 [B]
Typography by Stephanie Bart-Horvath
1 2 3 4 5 6 7 8 9 10 • ❖ • First Edition